GEMSTONES OF THE WORLD

SEARCHING FOR SAPPHIRES

TANYA DELLACCIO

PowerKiDS press
New York

Published in 2018 by The Rosen Publishing Group, Inc.
29 East 21st Street, New York, NY 10010

First Edition

Editor: Theresa Morlock
Book Design: Reann Nye

Photo Credits: Cover NIK/Shutterstock.com; pp. 4, 19 photo-world/Shutterstock.com; pp. 5, 12 Imfoto/Shutterstock.com; p. 6 MarcelClemens/Shutterstock.com; p. 7 Harry Taylor/Dorling Kindersley/Getty Images; pp. 8,17 Potapov Alexander/Shutterstock.com; p. 9 Albert Russ/Shutterstock.com; pp. 10, 11 NickKnight/Shutterstock.com; p. 13 Pann_Chucherd/Shutterstock.com; p. 14 GIANLUIGI GUERCIA/AFP/Getty Images; p. 15 Louise Gubb/Corbis Historical/Getty Images; p. 16 Demkat/Shutterstock.com; p. 18 ISHARA S.KODIKARA /AFP/Getty Images; pp. 20, 22 Pisut Phaetrangsee/Shutterstock.com; p. 21 Lukas Gojda/Shutterstock.com.

Cataloging-in-Publication Data

Names: Dellaccio, Tanya.
Title: Searching for sapphires / Tanya Dellaccio.
Description: New York : PowerKids Press, 2018. | Series: Gemstones of the world | Includes index.
Identifiers: LCCN ISBN 9781538328309 (pbk.) | ISBN 9781508164197 (library bound) | ISBN 9781538328361 (6 pack)
Subjects: LCSH: Sapphires--Juvenile literature. | Mineralogy--Juvenile literature.
Classification: LCC QE394.S3 D39 2018 | DDC 553.8'4--dc23

Manufactured in the United States of America

CPSIA Compliance Information: Batch Batch #BW18PK: For Further Information contact Rosen Publishing, New York, New York at 1-800-237-9932

CONTENTS

SAPPHIRE IN THE ROUGH

Have you ever noticed a sparkly blue stone on a ring, necklace, or bracelet? You may have been looking at a sapphire! Sapphires are gleaming blue gemstones that are often made into stunning **jewelry**. They're also the September birthstone.

Finding these beautiful blue treasures isn't easy. First, they must be extracted, or taken, from the earth. After they're extracted, sapphires are put through a process that makes them shiny, smooth, and ready to be made into jewelry.

Before sapphires are cut and polished, they're rough and dull.

NATURAL BEAUTY

All gemstones are minerals. Minerals are natural, solid **substances** that are not of plant or animal origin. Minerals are formed naturally, or without help from people. There are many different kinds of minerals, and each is made up of different elements. Sapphires are a kind of mineral called corundum.

Corundum is made up of the elements aluminum and oxygen. When no other elements are present, corundum is colorless. However, other elements may also be part of the mineral. This changes its color.

HIDDEN GEMS

Mineral hardness is measured on the Mohs' scale. Corundum is one of the hardest minerals. Diamond is the hardest. Mineral hardness is established by how **resistant** a mineral is to being scratched.

Colorless sapphires are very rare, or uncommon. They're also very expensive.

COOL CRYSTALS

Some minerals are created within igneous rocks. Igneous rocks are made of cooled magma. Magma is hot melted rock below or within the earth's crust. Magma may make its way to Earth's surface through **volcanic eruptions**. At the surface, magma is called lava.

As magma cools and hardens, it forms igneous rocks. Crystals may begin to grow inside the rocks. The more slowly magma cools and hardens, the more crystals form inside the rock and the bigger they are.

HIDDEN GEMS

A gemstone's weight is measured in **units** called carats. One carat equals 0.007 ounce (0.2 g).

A gemstone's crystal structure is made up of atoms. Atoms are the units that make up all matter. The atoms create a pattern that forms the shape of the rough gemstone.

THE CORUNDUM FAMILY

Rubies are the only other corundum gemstone. The difference between a sapphire and a ruby is its color. Rubies are red. Sapphires are usually blue, but any gemstones in the corundum family that aren't red are considered sapphires.

Different elements in a gemstone will make it different colors. For example, when iron and titanium are present in corundum, it will appear a different shade of blue. When the element chromium is present, corundum will range from red to pink.

YELLOW CORUNDUM

HIDDEN GEMS

Corundum gemstones that aren't blue or red are called fancy sapphires. These may be a number of colors depending on the elements present in them. Although fancy sapphires are popular, blue sapphires are more valuable.

Pink corundum gemstones are considered sapphires, but red corundum gemstones are considered rubies.

WHERE THEY'RE FOUND

Sapphires can be found all over the world. Their features may differ based on where they come from. For example, sapphires from Mogok, Myanmar, are often pink. In their natural state, no two sapphires are exactly alike. Some sapphires are found in rivers and streams and people must dig others out of hard-to-reach hillsides.

Many sapphires come from Myanmar, Madagascar, Thailand, and Australia. Sri Lanka is one of the biggest producers of sapphires. Many other kinds of gemstones can be found there as well.

Sapphires found in the Kashmir region of Asia are known for being bright and colorful.

DIGGING DEEP

Depending on the area, several different mining **techniques** may be used to find sapphires. Sifting is sometimes used to search for sapphires. Miners dig pits and sift dirt through screens, mixing in water to break the earth into smaller pieces. The sifting method is also used to find sapphires at the bottom of rivers and streams.

Other mining techniques aren't as simple. Mines may use large machines to dig up huge chunks of earth that are then sorted and washed to uncover the gems.

HIDDEN GEMS

Mining for gemstones can be harmful to the **environment**. In Madagascar, many animals and their homes are at risk because of illegal mining practices.

Gemstone mining can be risky–it's important for miners to follow special laws and rules!

TREATED, CUT, AND POLISHED

After they're removed from the ground, sapphires must be polished and cut before they can be made into jewelry. This process **transforms** the stones into shining gems

Many sapphires are treated with high heat. The heat helps **intensify** the color of the gemstone, making it brighter. Then, a worker called a lapidary uses several methods to cut flat surfaces on the stone to give it shape. After the gemstones go through this process, they're ready to be used in jewelry.

The word "luster" is used to describe how a gem **reflects** light. Different methods of cutting and treating sapphires can help increase a gemstone's luster.

SAPPHIRE CHARACTERISTICS

Each rough sapphire has different features that become visible when it's treated or polished. Some become noticeable when light reflects off the gemstone.

Some sapphires have what's called asterism, or a star effect. This is when a smooth gemstone has a star pattern on its surface that can be seen under light. Sapphires with the asterism effect are known as "star sapphires." Sapphires can also have a color-changing effect. This means that under different kinds of light the sapphire may appear to be different colors.

HIDDEN GEMS

The largest blue star sapphire was found in Sri Lanka in 2015. The owner named it "The Star of Adam" and has figured its value at $300 million. It weighs 1,404 carats (280.8 g)!

Breaks, scratches, or bubbles within a gemstone are known as inclusions. Asterism is caused by inclusions.

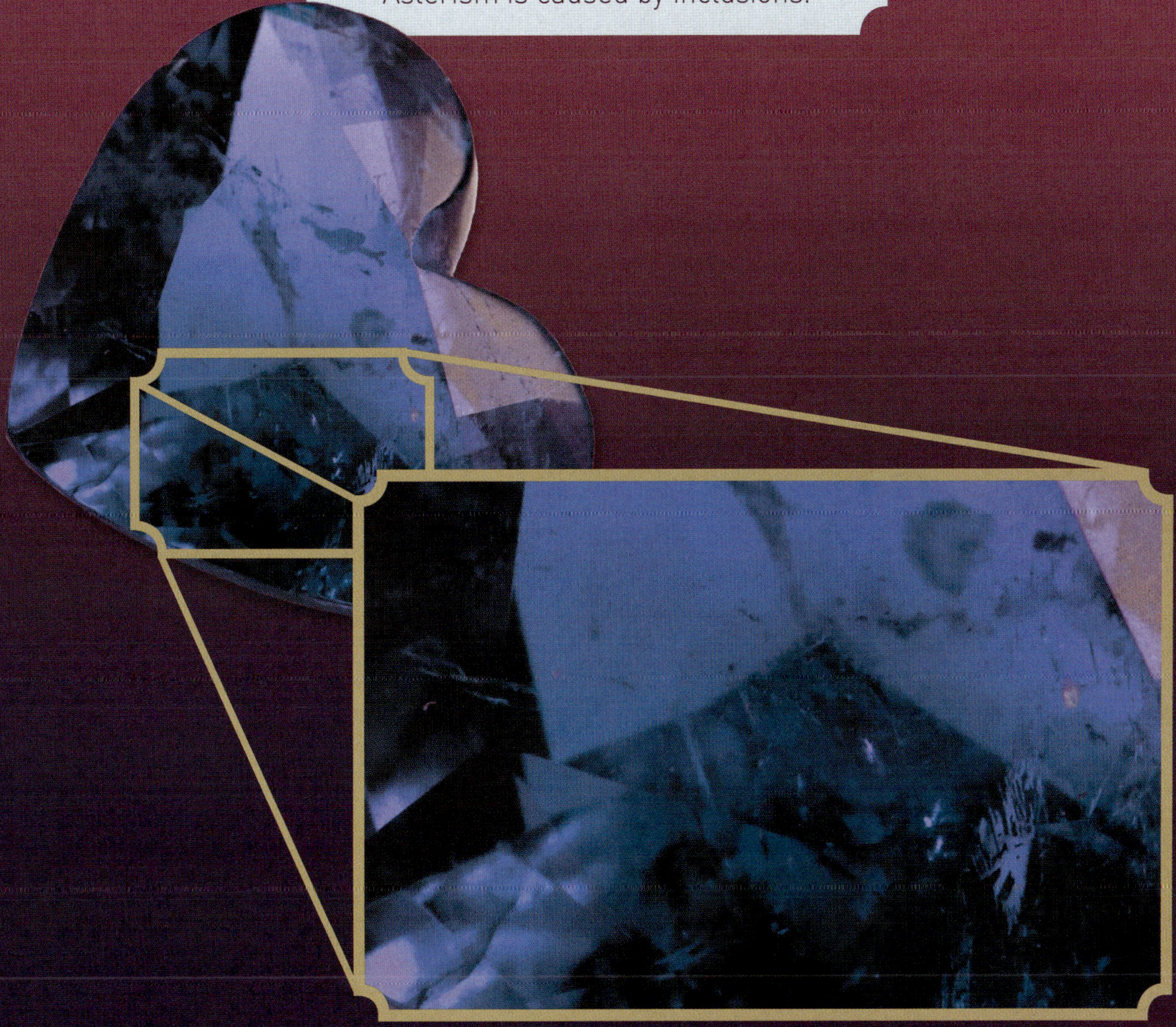

INCLUSIONS

SYNTHETIC SAPPHIRE

Scientists have found ways to create synthetic, or artificial, sapphires. Synthetic sapphires are grown in **laboratories**. They're created using the same chemicals and elements that make up the minerals in nature. However, they're man-made.

Although synthetic sapphires can be made in bright colors, they aren't as valuable as natural sapphires. These man-made stones have many different uses. Jewelry made with synthetic sapphires is more affordable. Artificial sapphires are also used to make many other objects.

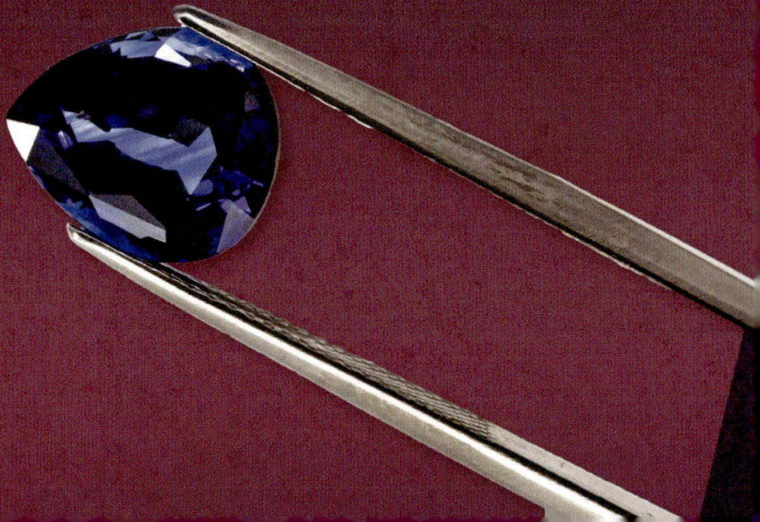

Synthetic sapphires are sometimes used in watches! Newer versions of the Apple Watch are made with synthetic sapphires.

STRONG AND BEAUTIFUL

It's no surprise that sapphires are some of the most popular gemstones in the world. The hardness of sapphires allows them to remain beautiful for years without breaking. Their bright, eye-catching colors are a delight to see. Though the processes of finding and treating sapphires are difficult, the end results are used to create priceless pieces of jewelry.

Since mining for these treasures can be harmful to the environment, it's important to buy sapphires from companies that use environmentally friendly mining practices.

GLOSSARY

environment: The natural world around us.

intensify: To make more intense, or strong.

jewelry: Objects people wear on their body for decoration, often made of special metals or prized stones.

laboratory: A room or building in which people do scientific experiments and tests.

reflect: To throw back light, heat, or sound without absorbing it, or taking it in.

resistant: Having the power to resist.

substance: A particular kind of matter.

technique: A method of accomplishing a task.

transform: To change into something new.

unit: A single thing, person, or group that is part of something larger.

volcanic eruption: An event in which a volcano, or an opening in a planet's surface through which hot, liquid rock sometimes flows, sends out that rock and other substances in a sudden explosion.

INDEX

WEBSITES

Due to the changing nature of Internet links, PowerKids Press has developed an online list of websites related to the subject of this book. This site is updated regularly. Please use this link to access the list: www.powerkidslinks.com/gotw/saph

TITLES IN THIS SERIES

DIGGING FOR DIAMONDS

DIVING FOR PEARLS

MINING FOR EMERALDS

RUMMAGING FOR RUBIES

SEARCHING FOR SAPPHIRES

TUNNELING FOR TURQUOISE

GRL: O

ISBN: 9781538328309
6-pack ISBN: 9781538328361

9 781538 328309

PowerKiDS press

Building Places to Shop

Community Helpers and BUILDERS

William Anthony